CONTENTS

Developments in society

When considering the challenges facing your company, a key question to ask is: 'Why would clients buy your products or services rather than those of a competitor?' Finding good answers to such a question is crucial. One answer could be that, when buying goods online, consumers increasingly want to buy from companies which are motivated by more than 'business-as usual' or the traditional 'bottom line'. Another answer could be that consumption is social, so that when 'buying' we take on the attitudes, beliefs, opinions and values of others. These attitudes are increasingly shaped by information shared digitally, often generated by people 'outside' of the companies which may suffer reputational damage and/or loss of market share. Hence companies that are unaware of changes in society run the risk of alienating customers. This is the case with sustainability which, despite being missing from most marketing texts, is increasingly important to key stakeholders.

If marketing is used and truly understood and implemented correctly in a business, it becomes a philosophy, a way of doing business – a whole approach, which should and must permeate throughout an entire organization. Hence, marketing is everyone's responsibility not just the specialist marketers who work in the marketing department.

FAQ: Why is it everyone's responsibility?

Well, think about it logically. How many times have you phoned an organization and been cut off or have been spoken to in an unprofessional manner or have not been given the answers you need? How often have you found a supplier's use of technology to be intrusive? How many times have you contacted organizations as a customer and been frustrated by staff who haven't been trained to deal with queries? Remember, not all staff are involved in sales and marketing – many are in accounts, logistics or 'tech support' ... and yet customers don't distinguish between the differing roles if they're dissatisfied.

The reason marketing is everyone's responsibility is quite simple, yet incredibly important – it's because we all play a part in creating the 'customer experience'.

FAQ: So, what actually is marketing?

If one word had to be chosen which epitomizes marketing, it would be the word 'customer'. Marketing is about understanding who your customers are, being able to anticipate what they require now and in the future and, ultimately, satisfying their needs. All the work your organization (not just the marketing department) undertakes should therefore be created and implemented to delight the customer.

The definition by the Chartered Institute of Marketing (CIM) is cited widely. It describes marketing as: 'the management process responsible for identifying, anticipating and satisfying customer requirements profitably' (CIM, 2014).

This definition is useful in understanding the key facets of what marketing is truly all about as it is direct, concise and almost every word in the definition means something that is critical to understanding exactly what the marketing philosophy entails.

Firstly, marketing is now seen as being of senior management importance – strategic as well as tactical and operational. For it to be truly embedded into the culture of an organization, it needs commitment from 'top' management. In many organizations today a marketing director will be seated on the board of directors to lead the organization forward through adopting a marketing philosophy.

Secondly, marketing is an ongoing process. There is no clinical start and end. It's neither linear nor is it a 'one-off'. It's continual – a process – it never stops or ends. As the world changes, so do our customers, hence our businesses adapt and evolve to move with the times.

As mentioned earlier, marketing is also about the future. Marketers must 'anticipate' customers' future wants, needs and values. Why? It may take your organization years to develop a new product (or service) and launch it into the market. Therefore, you must think into the future in terms of customers' perceptions and not just their current requirements. Increasingly, social media are being used as research tools to identify insights into how users (and influencers) see their needs changing in future.

If your organization can identify and anticipate customer requirements, you can move to try to satisfy them. But, once again, there is an added complication. Most organizations have limited resources: financial, staff, equipment etc. Therefore an organization must seek to satisfy their customers efficiently (with as little wastage as possible) and profitably! However, now more than ever, business activities should also be undertaken and managed in an environmentally friendly and socially responsible manner.

FAQ: Why focus on the customer and not concentrate on core organizational strengths?

The traditional view is that the customer purchases products and services from an organization in exchange for money. This simple exchange view is increasingly considered to be outdated. The reality is you can't 'give' customers value (a mistake repeated in many marketing texts). Some argue that the exchange brings the organization and the customer together where a co-creation of value takes place. Others argue customers provide money so they can seek value from your company and your focus should be on creating circumstances where they can seek and take value. These two options (co-creation and value seeking) represent less risk for your organization as they promote a customer-centric approach. Since value seeking and taking involves bringing (at least) two parties together, a relationship is formed and many marketers today try to capitalize on that initial relationship by finding out as much as they can about the customer and their needs.

Customers are also constantly changing and technology is enabling quicker, easier decision making. For example, consider the role of cost-comparison websites such as Gocompare.com and moneysupermarket.com, which not only compete with each other but also with organizations that 'represent' the customer (such as Which?). As customers change, their desires, needs and wants also change and if an organization doesn't adapt with them, the chances are that they will create dissatisfaction on the part of the customer and start to lose their customers to the competition. We call this customer attrition.

If the customer has a positive experience, they are more likely to tell their family and friends, and if they have a bad experience the chances are that they will tell even more people about it! This applies now more than ever: with the advent of Web 2.0 we've seen an explosion in the use of user websites (see **www.imdb.com**), blogs and social network sites (such as Facebook, Instagram, Pinterest, Vine etc). It is said that the one constant is change. While Facebook is still a colossus in social networking it's questionable whether it will be so in, say, 10 years' time. After all, how many people do you know who use Friends Reunited?

Consider the world we live in today. For many organizations, the marketplace is a difficult, dynamic, dangerous and highly competitive place to be. To be more successful, your organization must be externally focused, not just internally focused on production techniques, products and sales issues. A much wider view is needed. You certainly need excellent production techniques, products and sales initiatives but the need for awareness of the customer and other factors at play in the wider environment is paramount. Wherever and whenever you see changes in the market or environment, you must change and adapt, otherwise you risk being left behind and could therefore suffer quite serious repercussions. Many organizations suffer from this condition and develop a tunnel-like vision to their business activities. This is often referred to as marketing myopia – a short-sightedness that in this day and age can often result in the loss of customers and eventually loss of the business.

Nowadays many academics subscribe to Mintzberg's view that the business environment is changing at such a rate that we're all working in permanent turbulence and our intended strategies have little chance of reaching their intended goals without deflection (Figure 1.1). Therefore the marketing philosophy must be embraced irrespective of the size or type of organization.

FIGURE 1.1   Traditional marketing strategy being deflected by emergent factors

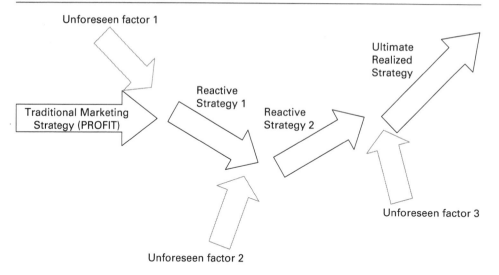

Example

Just think about what happened to Marks & Spencer (M&S) in the 1990s. This retail giant took its eye off its core customers whose needs were changing, the new competition that had entered the high street and the wider external environment, and, consequentially, suffered. Organizations seem to be most vulnerable after a sustained period of success. As individuals, we can become complacent when we are not challenged. It is unsurprising that organizations run by humans can react in an identical way.

Fortunately, M&S were able to make changes, which permeated to the core of their management culture and went through a process of recovery, where the focus of their philosophy changed to become one of identifying, anticipating and delighting the customer. They addressed social issues relating to supply chains and later led the way in adopting sustainable policies under their Plan A programme where they aimed for carbon neutral delivery of goods.

The rise of conflicting stakeholder interests

Increasingly, businesses have to meet rising public expectations and to address legal obligations around environmental and sustainability issues. The need for a business to make profit can, at times, conflict with its stated ethical aims and objectives. Hence conflicting stakeholders with differing needs, rights and obligations have to be managed.

Stakeholders are any group or individual who can affect or be affected by the achievement of the organization's objective (Freeman, 1984). However, be aware that they may only have interest in a project rather than an organization's corporate objectives. Certainly stakeholders can be deemed to be those who may benefit from or be harmed by the activities of your business. Where they can, to an extent, claim ownership in your activities they are deemed to have high power. You must be aware of the degree of interest and/or power stakeholders possess. A well-used marketing tool for mapping your stakeholders is the Mendelow grid (Figure 1.2).

FIGURE 1.2   Mendelow grid

		Level of Interest	
		Low	High
Power	High	A	B
	Low	C	D

Remember that mapping tools such as this are merely snapshots. It's always more useful to consider where the stakeholders may be in the future and (be prepared to) act accordingly. Stakeholders will have differing attributes due to combinations of power, legitimacy and also urgency. You will need to factor these ingredients into your stakeholder communications.

Corporate social responsibility

M&S changed their approach to business by improving their corporate social responsibility (CSR) platform (discussed in more detail in Chapter 2). Are your stances on these key issues available online or merely hidden in your annual report? Do you incorporate CSR in your mission statements? Do you refer to sustainability, eg ethical supply policies or charitable links? Are your policies transparent? Are they independently audited?

Where companies seek competitive advantage by abusing the reporting of their CSR practices, the reactions online are often swift and hostile! Social media sites can form the platforms for well-organized pressure groups to co-ordinate their communications efforts in order to influence corporate behaviour. You will need to monitor such sites and respond by clearly articulating your company's position. You can create a digital marketing communications campaign (marcomms or m-comms, discussed in more detail in Chapter 17) highlighting positives from your audits as well as how you're going to implement changes where needed. Many examples exist of companies that have benefited from positive word of mouth (WoM) by improving their CSR and in turn becoming increasingly sustainable.

It's worth noting that sustainability 'ownership' can be fuzzy in some companies and hotly contested in others. Some organizations recognize the importance of CSR with elements in their mission statements and may include 'green' issues (possibly, a quality control issue), ethical supply policies (the purchasing department) and charitable links (or all of the above!).

This corporate 'bun-fight' is partly due to differing approaches, eg what should be sustained, where and when? A way to address this is to arrange for cross-functional teams to contribute to your company's blog, wiki or social network site. Podcasts and vodcasts are very useful as your staff and other stakeholders are more likely to believe messages that come 'from the horse's mouth'. Remember responsibility may be shared between the service provider, the consumer, the community, the regulator and the government. This will be made easier by advocating and adopting sustainable marketing practices.

Patterns exist in the adoption of CSR across differing organizations. Companies that are highly motivated may adopt an idealistic stance or even one of enlightened self-interest whereas stakeholders on whom they rely may only adopt CSR practices when coerced. This potentially poses a risk for some companies; for example, Nike's poor PR due to allegations of child labour generated negative publicity that spread rapidly on social network sites. Reputations are easily tarnished by supply-side scandals with emotive issues such as child labour. Hence with your success depending on suppliers it's important ask yourself to what extent you can trust your supply network (a term preferred to 'chain') to act in ways you deem to be sustainable? Retailers, for example, are undoubtedly interdependent networking organizations and will need to trust their partners. Trust can be shaped by previous experiences and co-operative efforts and on the more general reputation firms build up. Sustainable marketers may also engender trust in like-minded consumers and that trust can be grown, say through PR, as a means of promoting positive word of mouth. Hence it's logical to recognize the case for measuring trust within your network.

FAQ: So what is sustainability?

We live in fast-changing times and it's not surprising that many terms are used to represent new concepts. Even terms you'd think were well established, eg the 'environment', are used in myriad ways in differing texts and in some cases by the same author. It's prudent to consider such concerns since consumers often connect with broader environmental issues. Their environmental interaction is important, intensely emotional and can affect their purchasing decisions.

It's therefore worth reflecting on key 'recent' developments that have shaped the sustainability agenda. The 1987 Bruntland Commission defined sustainability as: 'development that meets the needs of the present without compromising the ability of future generations to meet their own needs'.

In the late 1990s the issue was brought to much wider audiences (ie business academics and practitioners) when Elkington coined the phrase 'Triple-Bottom-Line' (TBL) in the *Harvard Business Review*. Since TBL was coined, the sustainable business development concept has grown, often being referred to as 'People-Planet-Profit'. This may still be new to many practitioners (and academics!), however elements therein have been practised for centuries. In TBL the traditional economic focus (ie the company's bottom line) is complemented by the addition of new foci, namely social and economic responsibility.

CASE STUDY   The Co-operative

One often cited example of sustainability in practice is the Co-operative movement, who have been practising recognizably sustainable retailing since the 1840s.

In 2009 *Which?* magazine surveyed 15,000 banking customers to find out who were the most satisfied with their suppliers. In the resulting first annual People's Choice report the Co-operative Bank and 'smile' (their exclusively online banking outlet) were amongst the top three overall winners when it came to customer satisfaction. Whilst, smile was awarded the highest customer score for their current account at 88 per cent, the Co-operative Bank followed closely with 82 per cent. The highest score for savings accounts was the Co-operative Bank with 80 per cent.

They ran into difficulties in 2013 when their banking division had to change in order to address a £1.5 billion black hole. In 2014 they had issues relating to their leadership, namely the appointment of 'suitable' leaders and also the CEO deeming them to be 'ungovernable'. This sounds alarming and possibly suggests that the member-driven co-operative sustainable model is flawed. That said, consider the following:

- They were (at the time) the fifth largest retailer in the United Kingdom.

- No senior management were found guilty of corporate malpractice.

- They addressed their financial situation without taking a single penny of taxpayers' money. This included selling their pharmacy chain to the Bestway Group for £620 million.

- They restructured their governance to improve decision making and implementation of changes whilst retaining their membership ethos.

- During the horse-meat in the food chain scandal not a single Co-op product was found to contain any meat other than that shown on the label.

- They retained high levels of member and customer satisfaction.

This compares favourably with many traditionally run retailers not to mention private sector financial services companies. The co-operative model has many exemplars around the world. In the United Kingdom, John Lewis is also a well-run members' organization that targets the middle to higher socio-economic segments. John Lewis (a socially responsible retailing partnership) repeatedly scores the highest mark for customer satisfaction with credit cards (90 per cent):

> Top of the table in almost every Which? credit card satisfaction survey since 2010, the John Lewis/Waitrose Partnership provides top-notch customer service and a product their customers are happy to recommend. In the April 2014 survey the John Lewis Partnership got a 79% customer score, ranking it 1st out of 36 credit card brands by a significant margin.
>
> (Which?, 2014)

The business of business is business...?

Sustainability is based on mutual benefit, ie both parties seek value and can work together long term. Milton Friedman challenged the idea of mutual benefit arguing that the *business of business is business*, ie a company's only moral responsibility is to make money for its shareholders (1970). He even argued that 'the social responsibility of business is to increase its profits', which somewhat dismissively alluded to the growing roles of social and societal marketing. Despite Friedman, more and more companies now espouse their green credentials whilst recognizing how a widening range of societal (ethical) issues has gained importance with consumers.

It has been argued that Friedman's 'Libertarian' position leads to acting in a non-sustainable way. Increasingly commentators think pursuing short-term profits over all other considerations contributed to the 2008 economic meltdown.

The sustainability continuum

Your company must be able to position itself effectively in your market if you wish to prosper. Hence you must know where you're perceived to stand in terms of sustainability. Assuming Friedman's viewpoint to be one end of a continuum, its opposite can be deemed to be 'pure sustainability', which is philosophical, arguably spiritual and wholly dedicated to improving the human condition (Figure 1.3).

This continuum represents how consumers and other stakeholders perceive companies. It's not about their outputs or self-projections, eg in annual reports. It's about how they're perceived and in reality consumers make simplified decisions using heuristics (which we'll discuss in more detail in Chapter 9) that reduce companies to 'good' company (say one with a good green or ethical credentials) versus 'bad' company (say one perceived to pursue profit at all costs). All companies are located on the continuum (knowingly or otherwise) and need to be aware of their position. Companies need to be able to position (or reposition) themselves within their markets in order to make effective decisions.

FIGURE 1.3   Sustainability continuum

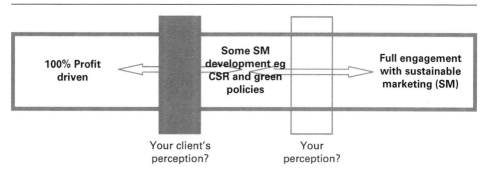

Obviously such tools are limited in that companies are complex and dynamic hence the continuum can only be a snapshot. That said, it's the vital first step. Two quick questions:

1 How do you rate your company in terms of sustainability?

2 How do your customers rate your company in terms of sustainability?

If your research shows that your customers' perceptions (of your sustainability positioning) don't match your own, then you need to implement changes. For example, if your self-perception is 8/10 and your customers rate you as 5/10 then you have a problem! You may be at a disadvantage – your competitors could exploit this! You need to know where you stand. If you have a poor rating you need to consider what's stopping your company from adopting sustainable marketing practices.

FAQ: Is sustainability a real concern for businesses?

Many companies have flagged their green credentials via blogs, fora and social network (SN) sites. However, just saying you're 'green' isn't enough any more. Your claims will be challenged. Companies that have sought to gain from (false) environmental claims have incurred the wrath of the online community which accuses them of 'Green-washing'. Simply put, companies that are not aware of the Web 2.0 driven changes in society run the risk of losing customers. So you need to respond to the new social media *and* operate in increasingly sustainable ways!

Elkington argued that the standard business-as-usual approach was changing as a result of seven 'revolutions' that were changing businesses' behaviours and leading to a more sustainable future. These revolutions are portrayed in Table 1.1.

Clearly, the 'revolutions' do not stand apart, rather they can energize or alternatively constrain each other. Nor are they chronologically linear or constant across different cultures. The complex nature of the revolutions is exacerbated by the (mis)use of the word sustainability itself. The best way to define and measure sustainability is contested. Terms such as 'ethical', 'organic', 'eco', 'green', 'fair trade' are used interchangeably when clearly they're not. In companies, terms such as corporate social responsibility (CSR), codes of conduct and sustainability are vague enough to gloss over big varieties in definition, stakeholder interest and involvement whilst at the same time being powerful enough to draw the commitment of many different actors, including consumers, other companies and (inter)national organizations.

It could be argued that 'business' is part of the problem not the solution. On the contrary, business needs to be at the forefront of the 'sustainability' debate as trade takes place (largely) between businesses and not governments. Hence it's useful to define what is meant by sustainable marketing.

TABLE 1.1 Elkington's seven revolutions of a sustainable future

Markets	Increased competition in more demanding, volatile markets making businesses more susceptible to the effects of economic crises.
Values	Worldwide shift in human/societal values making businesses susceptible to values-based crises when society finds them wanting.
Transparency	Increased transparency resulting from more open access to information, more authority of stakeholders to demand information, adoption of scrutiny and reporting systems.
Life-cycle technology	Acceptability and appraisal of products at point of sale loses significance and the focus rests on the whole of the supply chain from acquisition of raw materials, manufacture, transport and storage through to disposal or recycling after consumption.
Partnerships	Business partnerships will become more varied with campaigning groups entering relationships with business organizations once regarded as enemies.
Time	Sustainability issues lengthen time considerations making planning for sustainable business a matter of years, decades or even generations.
Corporate governance	Evolving corporate governance to include the representation of all relevant stakeholders not just shareholders, keeping the corporate board focused on all aspects of the sustainable agenda.

SOURCE: Adapted from Elkington (2004)

Sustainable marketing

In 2008 Gosnay and Richardson offered a definition:

> Sustainable Marketing (SM) is predicated on the tenets of the Triple Bottom Line. Hence SM decisions should be ethical and guided by sustainable business practices which ultimately are the only way to resolve the tensions between consumers' wants and long term interests, companies' requirements, society's long run interests and the need for environmental balance.

This definition should act as a springboard for your company. Sustainable marketing needs to be 'sold' on the basis of future gains and you may need to use a social media platform to improve your internal marketing in order to overcome resistance to change. Use it to improve your mission and vision statements. Then use your marketing communications (see Chapter 17) to ensure that all parties are aware of your position.

Sustainable marketing is an evolution of being market oriented (see Chapter 3) and largely uses the same frameworks and tools as conventional marketing. You will have to adapt:

- the information you use to make your decisions;
- the criteria you use to measure performance (sustainability audits may be required); and
- the company values, mission and/or vision statements with which marketing objectives must fit.

FAQ: Do the basic laws of marketing still apply?

There is an ongoing debate regarding whether the advent of Web 2.0 (featuring consumer generated tools such as blogs, price-comparison websites etc) has changed how marketing fundamentals are applied. Undoubtedly, the power of consumers has grown prior to making purchasing decisions and companies must adopt a more customer-centric approach if they wish to 'sell not tell'. It's not all bad as the benefits are not only restricted solely to the consumers, but also exist for your company. Certainly, you now have access to markets that may have been beyond your reach by conventional means.

Companies of all sizes can now reach millions of new customers on a global scale that, until recently, was available only to major corporations. It is the most exciting time there has ever been for starting and growing smaller companies and you can tap into this as long as you recognize that the customers' roles have changed and you need to understand how to let your customers either co-create or take value.

Think about this: many companies are interested in their customers' purchasing habits or preferences and have developed detailed databases to track purchase activities. Yet despite having customer relationship management (CRM) systems and mighty databases, the vast majority of new products fail in their first year. Why? Surely the massed ranks of marketers had sufficient customer knowledge to have a better than one in seven chance of surviving the first year. Apparently not!

Hence, more than ever before, digital marketing provides the opportunity to find out not only what consumers think, but also provides insight into the views of the networks and communities of users, prospects, friends, colleagues and even families.

Summary and activities

Key points

- Buying is always guided by consumers' thoughts, feelings and actions and since we take on attitudes, beliefs, opinions and values of others, companies which are not aware of changes in society run the risk of alienating customers.

- All companies are located on the sustainability continuum and need to be aware of their position in order to be able to position (or reposition) themselves within their markets by making effective strategic and operational decisions.

- You will need to operate in an increasingly sustainable fashion. Hence you may need to benchmark your current performance and identify (and remove) barriers to adopting sustainability.

ACTIVITIES

- It's worth hearing what Elkington has to say on matters relating to sustainability. Look up his podcast as follows:

  Elkington, J (2001) The Big Interview – Insead. Podcast via iTunes **https://deimos.apple.com/WebObjects/Core.woa/GetRSS/insead.edu-dz. 5565312238.05565312240?U=http%3A%2F%2Fwww.insead.edu%2Fpodcast%2Ft hebiginterview%2Fthebiginterviewvideo.xml** (accessed 1 December 2013).

- Review the Co-operative's world-class CSR platform (it is transparent, independently audited and they refuse to take business that contradicts their ethical policies) and the FTSE4GOOD and the Dow Jones Sustainability indices.

Digital marketing and research

Three of the most common areas of marketing research involve 'markets', products and distribution. Let's briefly consider each area:

- *Market research* – specifically undertaken on the market size, type, condition, volume or value. This research is particularly useful when you have the responsibility of researching brand new markets.

- *Product research* – focuses on the product, product features or desirability of the product. This is often used in the process of new product development (see Chapter 19) where the core focus of your work is centred around understanding the actual product(s). Alternatively, it can also be used if you start to encounter any problems with your products.

- *Distribution research* – where the products ought to be sold or, more importantly, how convenient it is for the customer to purchase the goods (see Chapter 18). During the development of an entire marketing strategy, the decision as to how to distribute your product is a key one.

If you are new to the area of marketing research, the important factor is that you truly understand what the focus of your research is to be, what information you require and what problem you are trying to solve.

The research process

Research (by its very nature being systematic and scientific) should follow a logical approach (Figure 5.1).

Let's consider the steps involved in conducting research.

FIGURE 5.1   The systematic marketing research process

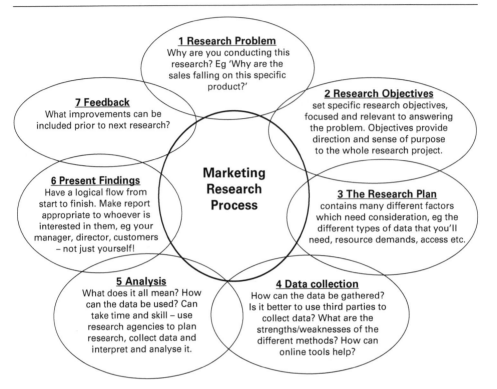

1 Research Problem
Why are you conducting this research? Eg 'Why are the sales falling on this specific product?'

7 Feedback
What improvements can be included prior to next research?

2 Research Objectives
set specific research objectives, focused and relevant to answering the problem. Objectives provide direction and sense of purpose to the whole research project.

Marketing Research Process

6 Present Findings
Have a logical flow from start to finish. Make report appropriate to whoever is interested in them, eg your manager, director, customers – not just yourself!

3 The Research Plan
contains many different factors which need consideration, eg the different types of data that you'll need, resource demands, access etc.

5 Analysis
What does it all mean? How can the data be used? Can take time and skill – use research agencies to plan research, collect data and interpret and analyse it.

4 Data collection
How can the data be gathered? Is it better to use third parties to collect data? What are the strengths/weaknesses of the different methods? How can online tools help?

The research question/problem

In order to define the research 'problem' or 'question' you need to reflect on why you are conducting this research. You will be trying to solve a particular problem or answer a particular question. Be as specific as you can about the problem or question you wish to answer. This is an important part of the process as it serves to provide focus to the research project. You can't afford to be too broad with your definition as this could create a research project that never finds the true data you require as you have cast the net too widely. Alternatively, you don't want to be too narrow with your interpretation of the problem as this could provide focus to a research project which does not cast the net wide enough to consider all issues that could be providing the problem – not easy.

Research objectives

Once you have identified the research problem/question, you then need to set your research objectives. Try to set SMART objectives (see Chapter 14) so your research is specific, focused and relevant to answering your research problem. Your objectives are important as they provide direction and sense of purpose to the whole research project.

Example

To identify if brand awareness of the Leeds Business School brand has increased amongst the West Yorkshire business community by more than 3 per cent year-on-year.

Create the research plan

The research plan contains many different factors; for example, the research structure, different types of data needed, resource demands, access and so on.

First, you'll need to identify the 'research design' that best suits your circumstances. Four of the most common research designs (sometimes referred to as methodologies) are:

- survey;
- case study;
- observation; and
- experimentation.

Please note that no methodology is better than any other. Let's briefly consider each of these.

Survey

Survey is used when the research problem needs a representative answer. This enables decisions to be made that can be applied to a larger population.

It tends to use questionnaires and largely gathers quantitative, numerical information. Therefore if you are collecting data that is based upon statistics to analyse, this is quantitative data.

Example

When psephologists Ipsos Mori carried out research to predict whether Scotland would become independent from the United Kingdom in 2014, they used quantitative data to represent the whole population of Scots living in Scotland. Scots living abroad, eg in England, were exempted from voting. They typically polled a sample of 1,500–2,000 prospective voters and generated results, which were accurate to (+/–) 3 per cent. When it's a close run thing, 3 per cent may not be accurate enough and they'd need a much larger sample or alternatively they can triangulate their findings with other surveys.

Case study

Case study is useful when seeking insight into how, say, an organization, a network, community or a sector behaves. This largely uses focus groups and/or interviews but occasionally smaller scale questionnaires. Case studies often collect qualitative or 'soft' data based upon people's attitudes, opinions, feelings or perceptions. Often how we feel is a greater force than how we think cognitively. Any longstanding football fan knows that the heart rules the head, particularly for the majority of teams who rarely win trophies! Qualitative research is often used to ascertain consumers' feelings regarding new products or services.

Observation

Observation can be used to collect data to gauge the reaction of customers to new products or services. Usually there is no direct contact with the respondent. Many psychologists study the difference in children's behaviour by watching them from behind a one-way window. They may introduce a new toy to the child to see if their behaviour changes.

Experimentation

Experimentation is where data is collected in controlled conditions. Researchers involved in scientific and medical research often use this technique as they can use controlled conditions in laboratories. By holding all factors constant and introducing one new factor, results can be collected as to the effect. Marketers could hold all factors relating to a new product constant and then manipulate the price at certain intervals to identify the extent to which sales are affected by increasing or lowering the price.

So, having considered some research designs let's consider the type of data required. There are two types of data, namely secondary and primary (ie data designed now for your purpose). Researchers often collect secondary data before primary data because it is cost-effective (it already exists), you do not need to be a skilled researcher to collect or use it and it is relatively quick to collect.

It can come from internal sources such as company reports or previous market research reports. External sources such as government publications, newspapers, magazines or directories are also useful. The internet enables secondary research to a greater extent than ever before although its scale is problematic with recent (already out of date) estimates of 65 billion pages in the web. Large research agencies, such as Mintel and Nielson, also publish research reports which you could purchase or commission. However, they can be costly.

This data is not specific to your research question, nor will it be up to date or particularly accurate, which are the key disadvantages; however, it may give you a starting point, or a feel, for the optimum direction.

However, the use of secondary data will only get you so far. As it isn't specific to helping you answer your research problem/question and because it may be out of date, and therefore slightly inaccurate, the chances are that you will need to collect more up to date and relevant data.

Primary data specifically seeks to answer your research problem and objectives. Therefore, it is specific, relevant, timely and if collected and analysed properly, accurate.

Data collection

There are different 'methods' you can use to collect primary data. When choosing the data collection 'method' you need to consider whether you need quantitative data or qualitative data. Remember, the choice (ie of qualitative or quantitative data – or perhaps the use of both) is governed by your problem and research objectives. You then have to undertake the collection of primary data, which is quite a skilled task with a variety of methods. Here are a few of the most common methods used to collect primary data:

- *Questionnaires* – a good questionnaire should be neither too long nor too short and should pose questions to collect the required responses to help answer the research problem/question. Generally, the type of data collected from a questionnaire is quantitative – you may not be collecting answers from the respondents which are based upon numbers but you will be able to analyse the data in a statistical manner. However, questionnaires do provide you with the opportunity to also ask open-ended questions to collect qualitative data, for example, 'what is your opinion on banning smoking in public places?'

  Questionnaires are very useful if you need to collect data from a large number of people. One of the key issues to consider is that you may not have the time, money or resources to question everyone. Therefore, you will need to question a representative sample of your target audience. Always remember, the more people you question in your target audience, the greater the degree of accuracy; however, as mentioned above, resource limitations may hinder you.

- *Focus groups* – another useful means to collect qualitative data. This is where you often select a number of respondents from your target audience, usually about 6–12, and ask them questions. Focus groups are very useful when you're developing new products (see Chapter 19) or services as you create the opportunity to interact with a selection of your target market and perhaps show them a prototype of the product. What do they think about its design? Size? Colour? Weight? Name? Etc.

- *Interviews* – in-depth interviews are as useful as focus groups to collect qualitative data. The key difference between the two is that an in-depth interview is just with one respondent. Therefore, the interviewer can really probe for in-depth answers, feelings, opinions etc. However, it is very costly as it is time-consuming and on a one-to-one basis – but the results are both timely and, hopefully, accurate.

Analysis

Once you have collected the data, whether secondary or primary, you then have to analyse it. What does it all mean? How can my company use the data? This can take time and skill, hence many marketers use specialist research agencies to plan their research, collect the data and interpret and analyse it. Quantitative data is easier to analyse as it's well suited to statistical analysis, spreadsheets or simple graphs. Packages such as SPSS or NVivo exist to facilitate complex analysis of large amounts of data. Qualitative data must still be analysed to identify themes and trends. Simply offering a few respondent quotes isn't usually enough.

Presenting findings

Once the analysis is complete, you then need to report the findings to who-ever is interested in them, eg your manager, director, customers etc. Rest assured that good knowledge gained from well-designed research can only strengthen your company's position so don't be surprised if others may find the results and conclusions interesting, so put effort into making the report stand out. A common mistake is that researchers and marketers make the report easy for themselves not the reader. Have a beginning, middle and end with a logical flow from start to finish. Don't start discussing things in the conclusions section for the first time!

Having considered the research process it's useful to reflect on how digital tools and platforms can help with your research.

Digital marketing research

The platforms, channels and tools made available through continued devel-opments in technology, and facilitated by the internet and networks, offer marketers access to a phenomenal amount of useful data, information and potential insight. But, as beneficial as this may sound, it can also present marketers with a significant hurdle, one that has only begun to present itself in recent years – the sheer volume of data that can be accessed; 90 per cent of the world's data has been generated in the last two years (Sintef, 2013). Individuals, organizations, communities and networks continue to generate data at an increasing rate, including areas such as our behaviour, communi-cations, interests and purchases.

The challenge for marketers has moved from gathering data, to analysing and interpreting it, in order to generate valuable insights and support effective decision making. Only recently are tools and processes being developed in order to make sense of the mountains of data we have at our fingertips – customer-centric marketing is becoming increasingly data driven.

There are two broad categories of data that marketers can consider – these are onsite and offsite.

FAQ: What's the difference between onsite and offsite data?

Onsite data is data gathered by analytics tools specific to the organization, such as Google Analytics, that track behaviour and actions specific to your website – traffic, journey, conversions and similar. Offsite analytics are much broader and focus on the potential audience, the wider population of interest, as well as sentiment and buzz and your share of voice.

FAQ: What are analytics?

These are the digital tools available to us as marketers that help us gather, store, interpret and analyse online data, which are become increasingly important. The use of these is also becoming an increasingly important part of the modern marketer's skillset. Research undertaken by Gartner (2014) found 42 per cent of respondents saw analytics, a key part of digital marketing research, as a top future investment.

Big data

Effective decision making is almost always underpinned by relevant data and the analysis of this. The focus on data has increased in recent years, facilitated by the innovations presented by the digital marketing environment, and there are an increasing number of categories, product data, mobile data, campaign data, website data, funnel data, engagement data, customer data, to name but a few. One category, or classification, in relation to data that is increasingly recognized and talked about in relation to more effective marketing is big data.

Big data is defined as 'high-volume, high-velocity and high-variety assets that demand cost-effective, innovative forms of information processing for enhanced insight and decision-making' (Gartner, 2014).

The key points to take from the definition relate to size, speed, complexity and range of data available. Big data:

- relates to big data sets, an increase in the volume of data generated, recorded and stored using technology;
- is fast, it is generated at speed and requires timely, if not speedy, responses to capitalize on the opportunities it presents; and
- comes from many different sources and in a variety of formats.

The challenges big data presents to the modern marketer is:

- identifying which data is relevant, which data actually matters;
- being able to analyse, draw out insight and react quickly; and

- how to bring all of this data, quantitative and qualitative, from different platforms and tools, together into a more standardized format for analysis and understanding.

A useful approach is to employ software that allows for visualization. Big data requires software for basic analysis, turning the mountain of data into more useful, meaningful results, and that can provide visual representations to support decision making. This isn't just analytics, it is the analysis of significantly larger masses of data, into the realms of peta- and exa-bytes. It takes a variety of data sets, from a variety of data sources, with varying degrees of relevance, accuracy and validity and gives it structure through matching, cleansing and linkage. It requires speed, real-time, rapid insights to help present opportunities that can be turned into competitive advantages before others.

Little treasures

In order to extract the most valuable, actionable insights from big data, organizations will need to have effective software systems (see Chapter 6) and be able to use them. As marketers start to dig around in the mountains of big data placed in front of them for the holy grail of insight in a potentially confusing and overwhelming environment, it's important not to forget the little treasures.

Little treasures can be found by tapping into existing data; the smaller sources of data you have more direct access to. Before moving on to the big data, get the little data right. What's being said on social media and YouTube about your organization? What do you currently know about your customers? What do they like? What do they do online? Where do they go? Can we link the two in any way? The small snippets of data and information we have are valuable, and shouldn't be lost in the age of big data.

Search, site and social

So, what data can we access easily? Where are the little treasures that will help inform marketing decision making and better serve customers? Everywhere! Actually, not quite, but it may well feel like that to start with. If we simplify the key areas (to start our online analytical journey) we can classify them into three Ss: **search** (search engine analytics and behaviour); **site** (website analytics and visitor behaviour); and **social** (social media behaviour).

When considering search engine marketing, we're not focusing on search engine optimization (SEO) and pay-per-click (PPC) but the behaviour of customers, and prospects, at this stage of their online journey. Customers using a search engine are often in the early stages of buyer behaviour, as covered in Chapter 7. They've recognized a need or want, or have a problem that they require a solution to, and they start searching for the answer.

Readily available data from Google or Bing Analytics can help us here. What we need to determine is what do they search for? What do they type in? What are the keywords or phrases? Those searching online are becoming more sophisticated in their searching, using longer search terms, or more long-tail keywords that are highly specific to their needs.

It is important to know where and when they search. What time of the day and in what location? Most searches used to be in a fixed location via a fixed device, but as we move towards a more mobile customer, and an always connected customer, knowledge of location and time can help us to determine readiness to buy, or what further information might be needed.

One of the most recognized forms of analytics and online research is onsite analysis via tools such as Google Analytic. You could consider alternatives provided by KISSmetrics, Adobe, Clicky or Open Web Analytics to name but a few, but there are costs attached to some). Onsite analytics provide insights into areas such as the performance of advertising, conversion rates, content performance and preference, interactions and flow of traffic.

Key things to consider are where our traffic comes from (so what inbound links and search engine terms are effective) and where they go when they leave us (not to a competitor surely?).

Also worth investigating are what platforms they use (desktop, laptop, table, phablet, smartphone, TV) and what browser. You can also see at what time of the day different customers or visitors come to the site. Are there trends in there? Can patterns in behaviour, with certain platforms, or geo-demographics, be identified. This can help us develop a more in-depth profile of our customers based on their online behaviour and preferences for technology.

Something else important is identifying and understanding what they do when they arrive on the site. What is the bounce rate? How many leave straight away? Which are the most popular pages? Do they relate to interesting or valuable content? What are their entry and exit points?

Finally, social media, asking similar kinds of questions to those in the previous sections of your data, even drawing on offsite data such as Facebook insights, Twitter Analytics or Social Mention.

Data we can start to build here paints a more psychographic picture of our customer. We can start to identify common interests, sentiment in relation to brands, purchases and experiences, even the stage of family life cycle and lifestyle choices. What is also useful to analyse in relation to social media is the frequency of posts, how active are they on different networks, and how much influence they have. Do people ask questions of them about purchases – do they appear to be opinion leaders or innovators in certain product areas?

Listening...

One thing that technology has really opened up is the opportunity for dialogue. Dialogue, as we marketers know, is an essential part of modern, customer-centric marketing – holding conversations, providing relevant content, posing questions on social media and creating discussions facilitated by hashtags.

There is a key skill required to be successful in conversation – listening. Social media and communities are fantastic places to go and listen (OK, when we say 'listen' here what we really mean is read and give consideration to). Good market research is about listening, clarifying and understanding – before using this to support decision making.

Bernoff and Li (2011) refer to this online environment, controlled by customers, as the 'Groundswell'. The Groundswell is a social trend, along communities and networks with individuals sharing information they want and need with others – avoiding organizations, advertising and other forms of marketing messages. Bernoff and Li recommend brand monitoring, listening to the internet. Who's saying what, where, to whom and (more importantly) why?

This is developed into a five-step plan:

1 *Who are your customers?* Make sure you have knowledge of who your customers are, where they go online, where they post things.

2 *Who are the creators and critics?* Who are the more vocal customers? Who has influence and impact?

3 *Start monitoring key areas – brands, products, service encounters.* Start small, focus on key areas and begin to grow your listening and monitoring as you become more confident.

4 *Draw on experience and skills internally; outsource if needed.* Utilize skills inside the organization: who knows the customer, who understands social media and online conversations?

5 *Have a skilled and dedicated interpreter.* Ensure that there is someone responsible for turning the data gathered into insight: what do these conversations mean, and, ultimately, how should we respond? (adapted from Bernoff and Li, 2011)

Some key ideas to start you off on your quest for useful data in the digital environment:

● Google your organization, your brand, your key products – but add in key words that describe opinions, behaviours, thoughts, experiences – use positive and negative terms.

● Set up Google Alerts – alerts can be set for keywords, names, companies, industries. You can control the volume of alerts, the sources accessed, language and regions. Google monitors the web, and when information, posts or articles are found linked to your criteria they're e-mailed directly to you.

● Set up Google Analytics for your site and enrol on Google Analytics Academy if you lack confidence. If you're not ready for Google

Analytics yet then sites such as Alexa.com and Similarweb can offer some useful data in this area.

- Visit free offsite tools such as Social Mention, Hootsuite, TweetReach and HowSociable. Use these to start to look for conversations and posts about brands and organizations – not just yours, but maybe your competitors as well?

CASE STUDY

In 2011, and updated in 2012, the concept of the Zero Moment of Truth (ZMOT) was introduced by thinkwithGoogle. The ZMOT is a specific online decision-making moment, the moment that a customer searches online and determines if what you offer will meet their needs based on the reviews, posts and information available.

Of increasing importance in relation to ZMOT is the mobile device, often an internet-connected smartphone. The smartphone is becoming a commerce channel in itself. In 2013, 27 per cent of all online purchases were made via a mobile device, worth approximately £3 billion (this includes both tablets and smartphones) (internetretailling.net, 2014). Smartphone sales grew 186 per cent in 2013 and are predicted to grow further in 2014.

Research on the go

A critical success factor in response to the change presented by smartphones and m-commerce is to have a consistent marketing strategy with optimization across all screens and devices. However, in 2013, only 55 per cent of UK organizations had a mobile optimized site (IBM, 2013), meaning there was no consistent strategy, and no consistency in communications.

Some companies get it right – Amazon, Starbucks, Macmillan – whether through an optimized site or a native app – but 45 per cent of organizations are still to realize the importance of the need for mobile-optimized content, or content that is responsive based on the device used.

Gathering data about customers and their use of mobile devices is important; this can be gathered via onsite analytics tools relatively easily. From this, highly usable, mobile-optimized content can be developed to meet the needs of those customers. If organizations aren't responding to this change, the mobile search for information and the potentially negative ZMOT when accessing poor mobile content, then you can bet a competitor soon will.

Summary and activities

Key points

- Marketing research is systematic in nature and a basic process is to be followed. It is used to give up to date, accurate information to help a marketer solve problems and lower the risk in important decision making.

- Many organizations fail to effectively monitor and conduct research into the digital behaviour and preferences of customers.

- Marketing research is at the heart of most marketing decisions. To remain competitive, innovative and attractive to the customer, we must constantly evolve our products, services and organizations. Marketing research is central to providing us with the data and information to help us to do this successfully.

- Advances in technology have had a significant impact on the amount of data available to marketers that can be used to support decision making.

- Big data is a term that applies to very large data sets, with a large volume of data, which changes and develops at a rapid pace and is drawn from a variety of sources.

- Little treasures should be gathered first. These are the quick wins – insights that marketers can gather from existing and freely available data.

- When starting to conduct research online, start by considering customer behaviour with reference to the three Ss: search, site and social.

ACTIVITIES

1 Create a simple information system in your office using past research projects, sales statistics, competitor information, pricing initiatives etc. Ensure that you file these documents (don't throw them away!). Even if you don't find them useful initially, somebody else might!

2 Visit **www.gartner.com/marketing/digital/** and register as a user. This will provide access to very useful webinars, blog posts and free research in and around the area of digital marketing and research.

3 Start to build up your knowledge about online customer behaviour with Google's Customer Barometer – **www.consumerbarometer2013.com/**. This tool provides insight into how customers use both online and offline information sources in their purchase process.

4 Download the *Zero Moment of Truth Handbook (ZMOT)* (**www.thinkwithgoogle.com/research-studies/2012-zmot-handbook.html**) and read the case studies at **www.thinkwithgoogle.com/collections/zero-moment-truth.html**. Consider the evolution of the shopper, or customer (presented by this study) in a changing digital marketing environment.

For more insight on big data access, see the following articles:
www.sas.com/resources/asset/five-big-data-challenges-article.pdf and
http://hbr.org/2012/10/big-data-the-management-revolution/ar